The words I would rather hide

Sofiya Terziyska

Presentation by *BookLeaf Publishing*

Web: www.bookleafpub.com

E-mail: info@bookleafpub.com

ISBN: 9789357440127

First edition 2023

ACKNOWLEDGEMENT

Thank you to my family and friends for the continuous support and understanding

PREFACE

From the author

With all my love to you, my dear

With "The words I would rather hide" I would like to encourage you to explore your feelings and thoughts but also to talk about them. Opening about your struggles without fear and shame will not make you weak, the opposite - it will give you strength.

I would like to normalise the internal conversation you might be having inside your head and to empower you to use it not for self-destruction but for achieving sanity and lucidity. Each poem gives different perspective about the challenges you might be having right now.

My missions is to raise your self-awareness, to validate your feelings and thoughts so you can recognise when you are in toxic environment or relationship.

Angel's demons

"Does angel have its demons?"
My soul has asked me once.
I've never thought of angel's darkest side.
Yet I felt it must exist.
Is it a real angel then when it has its own
demons?

Scattered leaves

Scattered autumn leaves dancing in the wind.
Breath taking sight in colours and shapes.
Order in the chaos or chaos in the order?

Are they ready to rest on the cold dark ground?
Are they willing to give up their colourful
imperfect dance?
I choose not to let go of them yet.

I'll keep all the colours in my scattered mind.
It's chaos in order and order in chaos.
So real, so surreal.

You can have it all?

3

You can have it all!
People like to say.
Yes, I can!
Yes, I try!
And I probably will!
But what if I lose myself in it all?

True colours

Royal blue suits her best.
How could she still wear grey?

Royal blue matches her skin tone.
How could she choose grey for the comfort?

Royal blue brightens her eyes.
Is grey not very boring and bland?

Royal blue truly is what she needs now.
How could she not let go of the grey?

Wildness undercover

I always thought I had more in me.
Wild inner child, full of joy.
Ready for adventures, laughing hard.
Running, jumping, searching.

But then I lost this sense of freedom
and my explorer's mind.
Where did they go?
Who robbed me?

I disappeared slowly, silently.
With all the goodness, brightness that I had.
Are they still in me but undercover?
Still alive but hardly living?

My wildness drowned in other people's
expectations.
Flooded by worries, fear, shame and anger.
Burned down by all the toxic people and
relations.
Crushes by the weight of hidden thoughts and
words.

Many untold, unloved, unlived stories...
Chomped by destructing teeth and voices
coming from all directions -
from inside and outside.

Once in a while I remember this wildness,
how a dreamt of more adventures and smiles.
I know it is in there,
waiting for more self love, understanding,
compassion.

Mind surgery

Trust me, he says.
Then he lies and cheats.

You only need me, he pledges.
Then he leaves her behind.

Smile at me, he insists.
Then he slaps.

Love me, he demands.
Then he kills – first her mind, then her body.

She wakes up in terror!

Bottled up

Beautiful house.
Laughter through tears.
Words full of silence.
Are you bottled up, my dear?

Walking

I've been walking in a fog for some time.
Nothing makes sense anymore.
Lost myself a few times.
I should be the same but not quite.

Who spread the fog around me?
Who keeps me there?
Foggy mind is confused, cannot fight
to protect itself from the dark.

My soulmate seems to be fine in this foggy
fields around us.
He insist is all fine and the fog is not there.
Then I disappear at the bottom of soggy craters.
I cannot see in the fog yet I keep walking.

Net

Frozen spider net
home to no one
scary sparkles
melting in the sun.

Why don't you shut up, babe?

It's been too long since I found you
In my heart, in my body.
You've been with me longer
before I was even born.

I raised you; I fed you.
Like a gentle part of me.
I needed you. Or I thought so.
You grew loud and noisy.

I lost control. You fought even harder.
I couldn't hear my true self anymore.
It was only you – the voice of doubts and
endless demands.
Never satisfied, never smiling.

It wasn't meant to be like that, right?
You had to give me hope for brighter future.
And help me wish for more, for better of it all.
To dream bigger, to become braver.

But no!
You conquered me from inside out.
And then you got too strong for me to fight you
back.
You tore me apart; you took me down.

One day I heard a whisper.
A simple melody.
Was it a dream…?
Or perhaps it was a memory?

So now with all the love I have,
I shout to you shamelessly,
my little demon of self-doubt and destruction:
Why don't you shut up, babe?

My answers

So many solutions, remedies, advice
on how to live my life
I couldn't hear years after years.
I wasn't able to, they weren't for me.
For back then.

So, I was fighting them all.
Hiding in my shell – it was delicate but strong
enough to protect me.
I was pretending that either I'm deaf, or not very
bright.
I have been watching how life has been passing by
In a struggle and silence.

So long I had no clue –
What's important to me and how to keep it.
And what to let go – with ease despite all doubts.
I couldn't hear nothing and nobody – not myself,
nor all other voices coming from near and far.

Now years later, I feel like I'm wiser
(But not that much more than before).
Enough though to hear myself. This little whisper
from inside.
I think I now know – who is there, what tells me;
What questions asks, where guides me to go.

So, now I look within,
where I'm silent again because I finally listen.
Listen to myself and hear all my voices.
Searching my very own questions
and giving my own honest answers.

Ashes

15

Can I be grateful for the flames?
Are they leaving just ashes behind?

Lost tracks

There are no tracks in the sinking sand.
Moving quickly around brings even more danger.
Can I stop for a while?
Can I hear the silence?
Can I stay with the feelings?
Can I embrace the good and the bad?
Can I see the first move?
Can I take it despite doubt?
Can I believe in the road ahead?
Can I whisper (or shout) to a friend or to a stranger:
"Please give me a hand!"
And to grab it, holding it still!
Can I wish for a saviour?
Can I hope for release?
Can I smile from inside out?
Can I make a small step?
Can I reach the hard rock out of this sinking sand?

Lesson

17

Who told you to smile when you are hurt?
Who taught you to hide when you feel like
running?
Who lied that the pain is okay when you love?

It's not too late

18

Silly people! They can't decide
What they really want in their life.

Actually, that's very good!
They ask for more. Search, explore.

Go out there! Don't wait till the end.
Enjoy this f*cking life. Before it is too late.

Escape

Empty shelfs,
broken glass.
Dark quiet room.
Sitting still on her own
but will not be lonely.

All the missing laughs

I don't want to miss any more laughs.
I want to enjoy every moment.
Yet still learning how.
I will not give up this time, or will I?

December

It's December. Another year slipped through the
fingers.
Year full of wonders, and worries.
Final rush but not until the end of the time.
Is there anything more to be done?

It's December. Children are happy -
Dream bravely, live for the magic.
No doubts, no holding back in their wishes.
Writing down, whispering all their desires.

How about you?
Been brave whole year?
Done good? Lived happily?
Smiled enough?
Dreamed for better life?
Said nice words?
Supported someone?
Loved with whole heart?

So many questions we ask ourselves.
And there is not right or wrong answers.
Same thing that could worry one, might be a
wonder for others.

We all hope for good but might do less, and
worse.
Not only for others, but mostly for us.

New Year, new "No"- resolutions

I can't wait for 1st January to start My New
Happy Year.
This time should be different, no vain
resolutions!
I have one wish - to say "No" more and often.

"No" to the fear that doesn't let me embrace
what I find in my mind and my heart.
"No" to the doubt that makes me stop before the
first step forward or upward.
"No" to the people that destroy me with purpose
or even without knowing the real me.
"No" to my thousands "No-s" every day that let
me believe: "You don't deserve better!"

My voice disappear...

Now what?

24

The beach is beautiful although it's empty.
The sea is there in the coldest winter.
Waves don't stop playing with sand, pebbles, shells
even when there are no footsteps and feelings.

Pray for snow

25

Cold hands in fluffy gloves grab the memories.
Freezing feet take the right path in the dark.
Dull eyes see home in the snowfall.
Silent voice finds the words in the blowing wind.
Smiley face peeps though the pain.